EVERY MAN'S GUIDE TO BUILDING A BUSINESS

HOW TO GET OFF THE COUCH AND GET *SERIOUS* ABOUT SUCCESS

ROBERT S. LOTT

LUCIDBOOKS

Every Man's Guide to Building a Business: *How to Get Off the Couch and Get Serious About Success*

CONTENTS

ACKNOWLEDGEMENT

There are many people in this world who have given me incredible business advice along the road. I could name them all and thank them individually for shooting straight with me. But there is no doubt in my mind whatsoever that my wife, Rebecca, is the primary reason I have had the business success I have experienced. She has ridden this rollercoaster with me the whole way and hasn't one time asked to get off. This book is dedicated to her because without her there wouldn't be a business, and we both know it.

EDITORIAL ACKNOWLEDGEMENT

I did not want to rush through the writing of this book because I didn't want it to be just another business book on the market. It required just the right person to help me finish it, and I was willing to keep looking until I found them. That person was Carol Jones.

Carol has a unique ability to listen to an author and truly understand the heart of the message they want to communicate in their book. She took my words and my thoughts, and my overall goal for this book, and she made it come to life. When she sent my edited manuscript back to me, and I read the last line, I was overwhelmed. It's exactly the book I wanted to produce.

Carol, thank you for your work. It's beyond outstanding, and I'm incredibly grateful.

Contact: Carol Jones,
Editor Benchmark Creative Resources
Carol@wesetthemark.com

PROLOGUE

YOU HAVE TO GIVE MORE THAN YOU TAKE

"The suffering and living on the edge of poverty and destruction feeds the soul of a true entrepreneur in ways that cannot be explained."

— Robert S. Lott

People ask me about business all the time because they know I've owned and operated some large companies. Not only have I owned and operated them, I have made huge amounts of money, and I've lost huge amounts of money. So I guess on some level that gives me a platform to talk to people about owning a business. I've seen both sides of the coin, and if there is one thing I have learned, it's this: I can give all the advice in the world to some people, but at the end of the day most people would rather be bitten by a snake than to actually step out there and do what it takes to start their own business.

There Are Easier Ways to Make Money

If you just want to make money, then go to work for a big company that has a performance-based bonus structure with an opportunity to excel because in that setting, you'll never have to worry about your next meal. If you're really talented and well-educated, you can go to work for a publicly-traded company and really get in there and work to your heart's content. If you're brilliant, they'll promote you and give you raises and stock options, and you'll make more money than you ever could running your own small business.

Or maybe you're not talented in a way that seems apparent to you (or anyone else for that matter), and you're not a brilliant personality, but you love just having a place to show up to everyday; you know the hours, you know the work, you know the life, and it's the life for you.

If any of these scenarios sound like you, then save yourself a lot of heartache and frustration and choose a stable job out in the work force. It's the best thing you can do for yourself, and there is no shame in that game.

But, if you're like me, then the road of captive employment just isn't for you. I was seduced at an early age by the mystery of life outside the box. Where most people chased the security of the tangible, I felt only misery when my life was governed by any kind of secure routine. I always have and always will be enamored by having the ability to write the script as I go.

That is the heart of a true entrepreneur.

For me, there's a magical process of evolution when a business begins to unfold and come to life; the suffering and living on the edge of poverty and destruction feeds the soul of a true entrepreneur in ways that cannot be explained. When companies are lifted up by the bootstraps through blood, sweat, guts, and integrity, the creator of that company feels and experiences something that few people will ever get to experience.

You have to think of it like this. Your business is like raising your children. If you go the extra mile and spend a lot of time with your kids, they'll wind up being functional human beings with a decent education who are able to contribute to society. However, if you ignore them and let them raise themselves, they become hoodlums with criminal records. A business is no different—you have to give more than you take.

You need to let those words sink deep into your mind, and if you decide that the life of an entrepreneur is the life for you, then you need to remind yourself of those words just about every day of your life. You have to give more than you take.

If you're ready to give more than you take, then I have a lifetime of wisdom to share with you, wisdom that will strengthen you and give you the skills you need to succeed as a business owner. But don't think this is going to be some sugar-coated-you-can-do-it business book. It's not. This book is about getting off the couch and getting serious about success.

In each chapter, you will learn how to succeed as a business owner through my own personal experiences, through the eyes of some of the most successful leaders in history, and through ACTION STEPS that will help you apply what you learn.

If this is the life you choose, remember two things: no looking back and no complaining. The arena of a small business is like the gladiator's arena in Rome, the distractions of self-doubt will get you killed in short order.

Are you ready to get started?

CHAPTER ONE

DO YOU HAVE WHAT IT TAKES?

"If you're just looking for enough money to hang out in the topless joints, look cool, and smoke Havana Cigars, you probably won't succeed."

— Robert S. Lott

Navy SEALS go through a grueling training, the worst of which is referred to as Hell Week. During Hell Week one of the most common sounds is the sound of a ringing bell, signifying that another SEAL hopeful has decided to quit and do something that doesn't require such tremendous commitment and sacrifice.

Jeff Kraus wrote in his eBook *You Want Me to Do What?*

On average, only 25% of SEAL candidates make it through Hell Week, the toughest training in the U.S. Military. It is often the greatest achievement of their lives, and with it comes the realization that they can do 20X more than they ever thought possible. It is a defining moment that they reach back to when in combat . . . Over the years, research has been done to determine a common trait in those individuals who make it through Hell Week, without a definitive answer. They are not necessarily the largest or strongest men, nor the fastest swimmers, but those with a burning desire to be SEALs. Instructors have observed only one true predictor of which candidates will ultimately succeed—it's those who want it the most—you can see it in their eyes![1]

Navy SEALS are known for being the best trained branch of military service. Their training and focus is laser sharp. They carry a reputation with them that says they are ready to

---

1. Kraus, Jeff. *You Want Me to Do What?* Navy Seals. Accessed January 16, 2015. http://navyseals.com/files/pdf/HellWeek-Ebook.pdf.

go, anytime, day or night, whatever it takes to accomplish the mission. But don't think for a second their life is sexy or easy. It's everything but that. And yet, it's all they can see themselves doing with their lives.

Likewise, the life of an entrepreneur is neither a sexy life, nor an easy one. When you first get started, you will feel excitement, sure, but you will feel an overload of self-doubt. And let me tell you this: your self-doubt will be nothing compared to the doubt your friends and families feel (and share with you). They will be in one of two camps. They will either think it's a hysterical joke that you think you could start a business, or they are certain you are committing financial suicide. You will hear ten thousand voices (most inside your own head) telling you why something won't work.

And for many, the need to have everyone on board with the decision to start a business will be the very thing that keeps them from starting one.

I get that. We all long for the approval of our friends and family in everything we do. We have been programmed to wait for permission and approval before we do anything. But if you're truly an entrepreneur, your desire to start something that is your own will override the voices in your ear and the ones in your head telling you that you don't have what it takes.

What Does It Take?

Starting and owning your own business requires a crystal clear vision and the willingness to face tremendous sacrifice. Part of your vision has to include understanding what you are willing to give up in order to get what you want. Are you willing to give up your vacations? Are you willing to sell off some possessions? Are you willing to get rid of all your toys—boats, motorcycles, the beach house, THE house? Are you willing to postpone getting married, having kids? What are you willing to sacrifice? What are you willing to give up altogether? You better have a really clear vision going in.

Unfortunately, a common vision among many young (and older) men I talk to about owning a business is what I call the Self-Vision. The point of the Self-Vision is to be self-centered and self-driven, which is always short-lived and will likely leave you all by yourself. When I tell you that you need to know what you really want out of a business, you have to be real with yourself. If you're just looking for enough money to hang out in the topless joints, look cool, and smoke Havana Cigars, you probably won't succeed. (I sure hope you have bigger and better goals than that!) My point is you can make some money, maybe even a lot of money, and buy all kinds of "things," but things won't last.

If the only thing you are working for in this world is to

buy a bunch of crap, then go get a job working for a big company that can pay you a lot of money. Because without some goals that run deeper than "toys," you won't make it as a business owner.

My goals were simple. I wanted to get married and have some kids. I wanted to make sure I had enough money for my kids to go to college without student loans. And I did just that. I made enough money and paid for both of them. I served 18 years on the local school board. I built a nice house when I was 30 years old. Those goals were how I saw myself long before I ever got there. I knew where I was going and what I wanted to do.

Remember those Navy SEALs that made it through Hell Week? They were sure of one thing, they knew they wanted to be a SEAL. Ringing that bell was not an option for them.

As a small business owner, you have to have that same kind of commitment, to do whatever it takes, no matter how hard it gets, to start and run a successful business.

There's No Such Thing

I think some people start a business thinking it's the easy way out. They'll make huge sums of money, work their own hours, and do what they want to, when they want to. Freedom. It's a word I hear thrown around a lot in the small business world. But if you're starting your own business because you want to come and go as you please, or get rich quick, you're in for a big, rude awakening, Jack. Once you start a business, while everybody else is out drinking a beer and hanging out, you're climbing the mountain. There's no such thing as free time anymore.

I remember with one of my companies in particular, on Sundays I would go to church, eat Sunday dinner, and hangout with my family a couple of hours. Around 3:00 or 4:00 in the afternoon, I would go to my office and work until 8:00 or 9:00 at night, sometimes later, preparing for the next day. I used this time on Sundays to call all of my construction managers and make sure everybody had what they needed to start work at 6:00 a.m. on Monday. I always discussed the scope of work on each project with the assigned manager at length, combing through the details. Conversations like those were crucial because when Monday morning rolled around, that was too late to start planning my week.

The art of owning a successful business is in knowing the details, and that's what people hate the most about business. While their friends are watching football games, playing golf, or just kicking back, entrepreneurs going the extra mile to reach their goals. Sometimes, they have to go a hundred extra miles over rough terrain just to break even. The life of an entrepreneur is a very hard life.

Ask yourself one more time, do you want wealth, or do you literally, honest to God, want to start a business because you know you'd be miserable doing anything else? You might discover you'd rather ring the bell, tap out, and work for a Friday paycheck, and that's okay. But if you're going to make the commitment to start your own business, then don't just sit there looking at your business plan. Pick it up, and get busy.

Action Step:

The first step to take before trying to start a business is an in-depth self-examination. You need to be brutally honest, because if you don't know yourself, you will never know your vision. What makes you want to own your own business? What are you willing to sacrifice to make this work? Answer these and any other questions that come into your head to help you be brutally honest with yourself.

The Take Away:

There are many reasons to start a business, and I am sure that you've thought of one. But, you better be brutally honest with yourself about the choice you are making.

CHAPTER TWO

BORN TO A LIFE OF
HARD WORK

"All of the successful people I've ever met seemed like plain, ordinary people. I never saw one of them walk on water or raise the dead, so I figured we are all equal."

— Robert S. Lott

I was born just before my parents' first anniversary. They were teenagers with few life skills or resources, and because of that, they faced many challenges in their early years of marriage. Getting saddled with me so early on probably didn't help matters much. I was the child from hell as soon as, I guess, I could talk. I had a very inquisitive mind and asked a thousand questions of just about anyone who would talk to me. The non-stop conversations drove my parents crazy, especially my father, a no-nonsense kind of man who didn't have the patience or the desire to invest much time in a boy like me. While some little boys ask thousands of questions about hunting and sports, my mind was never far from thinking or talking about owning and running businesses.

Oh, I had my heroes like all kids, but they weren't firemen, policemen, or sports stars. My heroes were the people who owned the pipeline construction companies that my daddy worked for. I can't remember a time that I didn't wish with all my heart to be one of those people. As I grew older, I began to realize how hard my parents had to work just to obtain the bare essentials of life.

They bought a small wooden frame house in Vidor, Texas, that had three rooms: a bathroom, one bedroom, and a small kitchen. My father sawed down several large pine trees that stood on the front of the property, hauled them to a sawmill, and had them sawed into lumber. With that lumber he built two additional bedrooms on to the house. He built all of the additions on that house at night after working a 10 or 12-hour day on a construction job. The man was not afraid of a hard day's work.

Watching him, I knew from an early age that I was born

to a life of hard work. It was a life I vowed to change with every fiber of my body and soul. I didn't know exactly how, but I was bound and determined to do it.

Working For A Friday Paycheck

My passion to one day succeed was strongly reinforced the summer I turned fifteen. I went to work with my father on a pipeline construction job in southwest Louisiana. We worked seven days a week for twelve to fourteen hours a day. The project crossed the marshy wetlands of the Lacassine Wildlife Refuge, which was covered in water year-round. We were riding home late one afternoon from an exceptionally hard day's work when I asked my father, "What do you think they're making off this job?"

My father sighed, tired and filthy from the work we'd just put in. He looked at me and said, "Boy, what nonsense are you talking about?"

"Well, if we're making these people money," I said with a little too much teenage boldness in my voice, "then we could do this very same thing, and we could make money ourselves." As I expected, he quickly changed the subject to the day's work or something far removed from business.

My father was a good man who came from a long line of honest people that had never known anything but hard work. There wasn't one person in his entire family that had ever managed or owned a business. He would, on rare occasions, talk about owning his own business, but like most working people, he never knew where to start. The risks were always a wall that he could never scale in his mind. I guess I always saw the benefit rather than the risk of going into business. That was the major rub and always would be in our relationship. He had several opportunities early in life to make money but he could never bring himself to quit working for a Friday paycheck and take the plunge.

When I was sixteen, there was a small rancher down the road from our house who had eighty head of prime crossbreed cows he wanted to sell at a bargain price. The man had gotten on in years and was retiring. The herd of cattle could have made my father a nice yearly profit with not a lot of daily management. I remember listening to him give my mother every reason under the sun why it was a risky deal. He didn't do the deal but wished a thousand times over that he had. I never could understand his mindset because when you're poor and living from paycheck to paycheck, what do you have to lose? Besides, all of the successful people I've ever met seemed like plain, ordinary people. I never saw one of them walk on water or raise the dead, so I figured we were all equal. They just had more money than us, but I figured I was smart enough to make some too if I kept at it.

That summer was my time to learn a lot about money.

BORN TO A LIFE OF HARD WORK

As with most of what's important in life, I learned it the hard way. The first day I rode to work with my father, he made it crystal clear that anything I wanted going forward I had to buy. From that day on, I paid my own way. He only gave me a place to live and meals. Any money he let me have after that was a loan, but he always made sure that every summer and holiday all the way through school, I had a job on some pipeline project along the Gulf Coast. The work was grinding for a young man my age, but it grew me up quick. I began to see the world through my father's eyes, and it motivated me tenfold to seek a better life.

The thought of working that hard for forty plus years for a paycheck on Friday that barely paid my bills scared me beyond words. He had hopes the hard work would push me toward a college education, which I tried for a while. I attended college for several semesters, but my mind was always full of schemes to make money.

My real motivation wasn't so much the money; I just wanted a better life for myself and for the family I would some day have. I wanted the sense of owning and managing something that I had created and built. I could never find any peace or satisfaction in working for a company from daylight 'til dark. Those kinds of jobs were a step up for my father's generation, but in my mind, they held little or no adventure.

Sure, I was born to a life of hard work, and I certainly

shared my father's feelings of pride in a job well done. But the one thing I knew about myself from a very early age was that I didn't want to walk in my father's footsteps.

Action Step:

Write a detailed vision of what you want your life to look like five years, ten years, and twenty years down the road. If it's not in brilliant Technicolor and playing like a movie in your head, then you are a boat without a rudder that is setting sail upon a dangerous ocean.

The Take Away:

Fear can drive a lot of men to miss incredible opportunities in their lives. When that fear sets in, having a clear vision of where your life is going will be the best tool you can have in your toolbox.

CHAPTER THREE

IT'S NOT THE SIZE OF THE DOG IN THE FIGHT

"Never let the lack of funds inhibit your ambition."

— Robert S. Lott

When I was 24 years old, I bought an old, run-down crew truck off a used car lot in Beaumont, Texas. It looked nothing like your modern white, four-door crew trucks. This was a beat-up, green, single cab, step-side Chevy with one cross bed toolbox that had been beat to hell and back. In all my life, nothing I ever bought or accomplished gave me such a feeling of hope and anticipation as that green truck did. When I drove that truck home that first day, my mind filled with visions of becoming the next major contractor in Southeast Texas, or maybe even the world.

My truck was paid for, so I didn't have any overhead other than gas and ice water. I worked odd jobs in the oilfield for several fly-by-night production companies around Southeast Texas. The work wasn't the hard part—collecting your money was the trick. But business overall was a lot easier back then in many ways.

My contractor's insurance certificate consisted of a forged certificate that I typed out on an old-fashioned typewriter. My two-man crew was an upstanding group who kept the water can full of cold beer. That was the order of the day back then. Sometimes they would be sipping on a cold one before the day was even over. The company supervisor we were working for didn't care because he was usually drinking by 3:00 p.m. as well.

I always paid my crew in cash on Friday, so I never had any payroll taxes or workers' comp insurance payments. (Which, for the record, I don't recommend.) The client's oversight wasn't as tight as it is today. When I didn't have contracting work of my own, I'd hire out to other oilfield contractors until I picked up another project. When I was awarded a bid, I'd go hire a couple of hands, load my truck, and go to work. Most of the work I did was building fences or just cleaning up around the oilfield locations.

A Bright Idea

It was during a time when I had my crew truck parked and I was working for my father-in-law that I had my first promising business idea. Well, in honesty, I really just copied it from my father-in-law. He hired me to run an excavator unloading railcars of limestone that he was shipping into Southeast Texas.

I saw what he was doing and recognized there weren't many aggregate suppliers along the Gulf Coast. This was during the late seventies and the oilfield was starting to heat up, red hot. The demand for road aggregate was like a lot of other products and services back then. The purchasing agents in the industry were more interested in delivery than price. The market conditions were perfect for a startup business, especially in the aggregate business. Because aggregate products had a variety of applications in the construction industry, my father-in-law was a real innovator. He found new ways to use limestone rock to build heavy haul roads in the oilfields around Beaumont, Texas. I learned a lot about business working for him, some good, some not so good, but I guess the point is, I was always learning.

After working for him for about a year, I started looking along the Gulf Coast for a place to open an aggregate yard of my own. Looking at the market, I saw a huge expanse of undeveloped land in and around the refineries in East Houston. I did a little research and looked around at other towns in Texas. Basically, all of the towns in Texas seemed to grow to the west and northwest. Everything industrial— the majority of it—was built on the east and south side of the major metropolitan area. So, I figured the east side of Houston was going to experience a huge industrial growth in years to come. The problem was that I couldn't find anything to lease. I drove all over the east and south side of Houston looking for a rail siding and couldn't find one available track.

My younger brother, Jeff, was living with me at the time, so we decided to join forces and look for a place to open an aggregate business in Houston. He was 20 at the time, and I was 28. The only thing we had between us was a clear vision, and I mean the only thing, because our resumes consisted of zero business experience and zero financial resources. This lack of experience and money was really a blessing because we were standing on rock bottom. Where did we have to go but up? So we embarked upon a single-minded quest to go into the aggregate business.

That's when I had a bright idea. I thought, "We'll go down to the local airport and rent a light plane." I figured we could fly over the area and see the potential market plus understand how the railroads operated in Houston.

We could also identify all of the unused or abandoned rail sidings. When we finally found a charter service, we barely had enough money for a short flight over East Houston.

We loaded up in this little plane and flew all over the east side of Houston following all of the different rail lines. We took lots of notes on where all of the heavy industry was located and how the rail traffic moved. I was totally amazed at all of the undeveloped land that was on the east side of Houston and north of the ship channel.

As we were flying around, I noticed a rail spur that turned off the main line in Channelview, which was on the east side of Houston. It was located just off of a long set out track, which was perfect for rail cars of limestone. The spur turned into a large tract of land that was heavily overgrown in trees and brush. The rail spur disappeared beneath the overhanging trees that grew next to the track. I told the pilot, "I've seen what I need." It was a good thing because our flying time was almost up.

Taking On the Missouri Pacific Railroad

When we got back to our truck, we drove back to where the rail spur had disappeared and followed it into the woods. The track was completely covered in weeds and briars, but to my disbelief the rail and ties were in perfect condition. Early the next day, we were in the Harris County Tax Office researching the tax rolls to see who owned the land and rail spur.

Remember, being an entrepreneur requires you to think outside the box, to educate yourself where you lack education, and to stop at nothing to get the answers you want.

We found out that the first tract of land alongside of the rail was 26 acres of heavy timber that was owned by a company in North Texas. The rail spur and four acres that bordered on Sheldon Road were owned by the Missouri Pacific Railroad. The railroad's property was in worse condition than the adjoining 26 acres because it was not only overgrown with trees, but it was also covered in about four feet of garbage.

It took us several visits to the Missouri Pacific office in Houston before we found the right person to talk to. When we finally got an appointment to see him, I asked him to lease us the four acres of land, including the rail spur. His answer came two seconds later: the railroad had no interest in any more rail traffic in the area.

The average person would have probably just walked away, but I was way too hard-headed and stubborn to give up that easily.

I left the office thinking, "If we could somehow lease that four acres, clean it up, and start doing business, we just might get a chance to buy that 26 acres and build a big train-unloading facility." But first, we had to figure out a way to convince the railroad to lease it to us. They were steadfastly uninterested in any new business in the area.

After several more trips to the railroad office, we found out that the train master, who is over the rail system in that particular area, didn't want any more traffic on that part of the railroad. He couldn't deny us service if we built our own track, but he could stop the real estate department from leasing us the company-owned rail and property. When we first approached him about reconsidering his decision, he dismissed us both like we were kids playing in his train yard. In fact, I will never forget the look on his face as we introduced ourselves to him. He had heard our name on several occasions, but we had never met. After the introductions and shaking hands he stood there looking us both over trying to contain himself. The disrespectful way he treated us was like the first taste of blood in your mouth during a fight. It was the best thing that could have ever happened to me, because it brought me back to the real world. When you first start a business (at any age) you get lost in all the possibilities of grandeur and wealth. You ponder your legacy and how you'll write your name in the history books of business. Stop right here and let me bring you back to the real world. Don't be the naïve fighter walking to the ring on fight night thinking about your victory celebration and all of the good-looking women who'll be trying to catch your eye. There has never been a victory gained that didn't come with a beating and sometimes several beatings. So train hard and be prepared for when you step into that ring. There has never been a fighter that held that world championship belt above his head after a fight that wasn't exhausted and beat to a pulp. The business world is no different from the ring. There will never be any easy victories. So learn to savor the taste of blood; it's a reminder that there is a victory to be had.

With the Missouri Pacific Railroad, I had tasted blood and wasn't ready to take 'No' for an answer. Five days a week, we were standing at the front door of the Missouri Pacific Office Building in downtown Houston when the doors opened for business. We would politely walk in with the railroad employees and sit down in the lobby, where we sat for the majority of the day, every day.

That routine went on for weeks on end. The real estate guys all knew why we were there, but no one else seemed to particularly care. This was a long time before terrorists and gun nuts, when odd people like us were just part of the everyday scenery.

After several weeks, we became pretty good friends with several of the guys in the real estate department. As they came through the lobby they'd say, "Hey Robert, Jeff, what's going on? Come have a cup of coffee with us." And of course we followed them down to the kitchen where we talked about everything under the sun, everything *except* railroads.

There's No Plan B

There were many days when I just wanted to go home and forget the whole aggravating business, but something just wouldn't let me quit. I had a feeling in my gut that somehow we were going to get a deal with the railroad. Besides, when I looked at my life, the only ray of hope I had was that garbage dump of four acres. Our options were zero, so what did we have to lose?

One day while we were sitting in the lobby, the main man in charge of all the industrial property for the Missouri Pacific Railroad walked out and abruptly summoned us to his office. He was an older gentleman, probably late fifties or early sixties, and walked like a man who'd spent too many years sitting at a desk pushing paper. I was dumbfounded that we were actually being invited to his office. Jeff and I traded looks of doom as we followed him down the hall. We both thought that this would be the day he would run us out of the building once and for all. As we walked in, he said, "You boys are just bound and determined to do this deal, aren't you?"

"Well, you know," I said, "we don't have a Plan B. We need that land and that's all there is to it."

We explained our vision for the property and how we wanted to develop the rail and surrounding property. After we finished, he sat there silently for a moment. Unconsciously, I held my breath, thinking we had wasted our time and his. Then he said, "I talked to some of our people, and I've recommended they lease you the four acres and track. We're evaluating the terms." We were spellbound, and couldn't speak for several moments.

Finally, I realized I had been holding my breath and exhaled slowly as I spoke, my voice coming out a little bit higher pitched than I had planned. "Really?" I choked out. Then I quickly cleared my throat and added, "Well, before we go any further, let's understand something. We don't have a lot of money."

The old man laughed and said, "Well, from the looks of you boys, we figured that."

He agreed to lease it to us very reasonably with the understanding that once we cleaned up the property and got into business, the lease would escalate. We shook his hand and said, "That's fair. Just let us clean it up and go to work. And when we start shipping lots of rail cars, we'll pay you a whole lot more money." I left that office with a sense of accomplishment I have rarely felt since. Who would have ever thought that a couple of raggedy kids from East Texas could make such a deal?

So, believe it or not, after one week of working out the

terms, we had the lease in our hands. That's when I realized what we really had. It's kind of like hemming a grizzly up. You get the bear hemmed up and then you have to figure out what you're going to do with him. Between sweating, and thinking, and praying you don't get eaten alive, you figure things out.

That's how it is in business. You spend most of your time in the swamp up to your neck in alligators praying not to get eaten while you figure how to drain the swamp. But **that** is exactly where you want to be. When your life is on the line (your personal and financial life) that's when you get real smart about how to run a successful business.

A Lot of Drive and a Lot of Fight

The first day, Jeff and I drove up to the property and got out of the truck. We stood there in silence staring at all of the garbage and dense woods that grew right up to the rails. We looked at each other and almost started laughing. Jeff more to himself than me said, "What now?" I replied, "I don't know, but let's find some equipment and get to work."

We looked around and found an equipment dealer not far down the road. I went down to this guy's office, Smith Equipment Rentals, and talked to the owner about renting some equipment. I said, "We have a piece of property down the street, and we're opening a business."

"My problem is we need a bulldozer because our property is heavily wooded with lots of garbage everywhere. We need to get it pushed and burned. Then I need an excavator to load everything that doesn't burn into trucks and haul it off."

After the guy gave me his prices, I said, "Well, I have this other problem. We don't have much money." Like I said, never let the lack of funds inhibit your ambition.

The owner looked at me and said slowly, "I see."

We had just taken on the Missouri Pacific Railroad and walked away with a deal no one would have ever believed possible. So you can bet there was no way I was walking away from this guy without the equipment we needed. I looked at him and said in my most convincing voice, "I'll make you a deal. You have a big equipment yard that's covered with aggregate. You let me have the bulldozer and the excavator, and we'll sign a rental ticket. Then, when we get into business, we'll give you limestone aggregate back a little bit along the way until we're square."

He looked at me and smiled. "You got guts kid," and he shook my hand. And just like that, we had what we needed to run our first business.

I still look back at that first business and am amazed at what we accomplished at such a young age. I think one of the most important things I learned early on was that I could find a million excuses not to do something. I could have said I didn't have money, because I didn't have money, but I didn't let that stop me. I didn't let my age stop me. I didn't let my inexperience stop me. I didn't let a million naysayers stop me.

Jeff and I had a whole lot of things against us and only one thing in our favor. We had a lot of ambition, a lot of drive, and a lot of fight.

There is an old East Texas saying that my step-grandpa used to quote to me regularly when I was a kid growing up. He said, "It's not the size of the dog in the fight - it's the size of the fight in the dog." My brother and I are living proof of that.

Action Steps:

1. Constantly be thinking of your vision even when there is no measurable forward motion. If you are already in business for yourself, are you sensing there is no forward motion? If not, when was the last time you measured your business progress against your vision?

   Write down what next steps you need to take to create some forward motions.

2. Be creative in solving your problems.

   Find a quiet place to write and think. Make a list of every possible solution you can think of, even the crazy ones. Learn to think out of the box. Remember that being creative is a skill that must be practiced daily.

The Take Away:

One hundred percent of all entrepreneurs always need more resources than what they start off with. Don't let that limit you.

CHAPTER FOUR

LET YOUR ACTION DEFINE YOUR PASSION

"Passion is striving to make your life the best it can be in all aspects: mentally, physically, spiritually, and financially."

— Robert S. Lott

The main reason the railroad leased me the land at the beginning of my career was that one guy saw the passion in me. He saw my driving force and he understood, "If I lease this to him, it's an advantage to the railroad. It's revenue. It's sales, and his passion is going to make me some money."

If I'd gone in there and had no real plan or passion for what I wanted to do with it, there's no way I could have walked out with the lease. When the day came that he finally asked me, "What are you going to do with this?" I said, "We're going to open an aggregate business and run a lot of unit trains there. We're going to sell a huge volume of rock. It's going to be a very good revenue stream for the railroad." I said it in a way that left no room for doubt. People have to know that you are all in before they'll go out on that limb for you. No one will want to do business with somebody that isn't all in.

I had a young man come to my office one time looking for some help getting started in business. I asked him if he wanted something to drink, and I'm not kidding you, it took that kid a good two minutes to decide what he wanted to drink. At one point he even asked me, "What are you having?" I knew then and there I wouldn't be helping him. If you can't even decide what you want to drink without overthinking it, there's no way you're going to be able to make critical decisions on the fly.

You need to remember that people are busy these days. They want to help you, but they don't have time for someone who isn't sure what they want or how to go about getting it. So be decisive in everything you do. Don't let someone else be out in front of you making your decisions for you.

Michael Jordan didn't become Michael Jordan because others decided he would be great. That's not what he did. He lived in the moment and wore his passion and competitiveness on his sleeve. It's what he was. It was practically tattooed over his whole body.

The only decisions you believe in are the decisions you make yourself.

To excel at the top of any field, you have to be all in—physically, mentally, and financially. Your personal relationships and everything in your life have got to be in the backseat—they have to be second place to that passion.

If you want to be successful, you have to define yourself by your passion.

Be Passionate. But Don't Be Stupid.

There are two things that fuel the heart of an entrepreneur: the unbridled desire to create something from scratch, and the pure adrenaline rush that comes from stepping out there on your own. Just as your passion will carry you far in business, it can also carry you too far.

In the late 1970's when Carter was in office, we came out of the gas shortages and the oil field went on a roll. That whole oil field boom was just incredible. Everybody thought that they would never see another poor day. Economists can tell you that the American economy cycles on economic curves every few years, and we were on a high point in that curve. I was young, just 30 years old when it really began to move in 1980, and I wanted to take advantage of it.

My brother and I made more money than we knew what to do with during that late seventies to early eighties boom. One unforgettable day, we were in the back of our train yard working when I saw a Mercedes coming through the yard toward us. Turns out it was a carload of bankers out driving around making sales calls. They pulled up, got out, and introduced themselves. They asked if we had a few minutes to visit with them about some real lending opportunities. We said sure, so we all went back up to our office and sat down. The lead guy of the group was probably in his early sixties, gray-haired, very distinguished, with a big college ring. He had two young guys with him, early thirties that were pure type A, bone-eaters.

After about an hour of chitchat and answering a few basic questions about our business, I turned to the gray-haired man and said, "You've seen our yard and know generally what we do. What kind of money do you think you would loan a couple of guys like us?"

He answered, "Ah, I don't know. We probably could set a line up for four or five million."

My brother and I both looked a little dumbfounded. I

finally smiled and said, "Thank you, but we're really not interested in borrowing any money. We don't want to be over-leveraged and in debt in case something goes wrong."

He jumped right back in with his authoritative banker's voice and said, "Well, I understand that, but things are booming. The market is red hot. Think of what you could do with four to five million dollars. Think of the staggering returns you could make with that kind of available cash."

After they got up and left our office, I said to my brother, "Shut that door a minute and let's talk. There is something seriously wrong with the world today, and I mean seriously wrong. In fact it's downright insane."

I knew he was thinking the same thing, but he asked, "Why is that?"

"Because I'm dirty from head to toe, wearing a pair of worn-out blue jeans, and you're dressed no better. We look like two day laborers and here comes this high-powered banker with all kinds of experience that wants to loan us four or five million dollars. And on top of that he drives out here to see us? There's some serious lending going on out there to people who can't pay it back, and somewhere there has to be a train wreck."

In that moment, I was clear-headed and didn't let my passion get us in over our heads. But eventually, like everyone else in the oil and gas business, we overbuilt.

We greedily stepped off the top of Everest, and, in 1983, the crash hit. It didn't kill us, but we had to sell a lot of assets. We weren't quite over-leveraged because we owned almost everything we had. We probably had about four million dollars' worth of assets, and we owed about one million dollars on them. We sold everything we had for one million dollars, and we kept just a few pieces of equipment to make a living with. We moved to the oilfields in deep East Texas and went to work building roads and running equipment for the next few years until the economy rebounded.

There are always repercussions to passion if you're not careful with it, especially during an economic boom. The industry becomes over-aggressive and over-confident and it's hard not to get caught up in all the hype.

Passion for the Right Things

The first five years my wife and I were married, we didn't have any children. We didn't have the money or the time for kids. It was all we could do with the both of us working just to make ends meet. When it comes to owning your own business, you have to prioritize and balance your life. Make sure your passion is placed where it counts, and the people that matter will understand. Work your guts out, and when you are done, give all you can to your wife and kids. Your family will live with that; just make sure you don't put anything else out ahead of them.

I remember there was a time in my life when all I wanted to do was be a rodeo cowboy. I soaked it in. I did everything I could think of doing to be the best rodeo cowboy I could be. But, one day I realized it was a great hobby, but I could never make a living for my family as a rodeo cowboy. So I up and quit, and I mean quit. It is a hobby that I have enjoyed for many years, but it is just that—a hobby. I walked away *for one reason,* because it wasn't what I was meant to do with my life, and I knew it. I was ten to one better at running a business than I ever would have been trying to rodeo for a living. If I had tried to rodeo plus run my business, it wouldn't have been long before I lost everything, including my wife. Asking your family to suffer for something that doesn't benefit everyone is clearly a selfish motive. I quit because my passion for my wife and family was stronger than my passion to be a rodeo cowboy. My actions proved that my passions were in the right place. But it could have easily gone the other way if I hadn't been very clear about my vision earlier on in my life.

When you start making a boatload of money, it will get real easy to get your priorities out of order. I've seen it happen a million times. It'll cause you to live your life counter to your obligations. I can't have time for my business and time for my personal hobbies and all the little things I want to go do, only to let my family suffer. If your family and your wife get too far down and stop believing in your passion, they're not going to stick around and be there for you.

Let your action reflect your passion in life.

Action Step:

Draw a target on a piece of paper. In the center ring, write your name. Now in the other rings, write what is important to you in your life. What are the things in your life that matter most to you? Use this as a guide on your best days and on your worst days to make sure your passion is for the right things.

Take Away:

You can control two things in business: how you start, and how you finish. The crooked road in between is just that, a crooked road. Be passionate about what's important and decisive about how you're going to get it.

CHAPTER FIVE

WALKING THE TIGHTROPE

"When you feel that gut-wrenching fear in the pit of your stomach, it's how you know you're going to fight to succeed."

— Robert S. Lott

n 1920, a young teenager named Karl Wallenda answered an ad that simply read, "Hand balancer with courage needed for circus work." Karl had been born into the circus and as any adrenaline driven teenage boy would do, he jumped at the chance to do something risky and adventurous. Almost ten years later, Karl and his handpicked team arrived at Madison Square Garden with the Ringling Bros. Circus and walked the tightrope without a net for the first time in history (because the net had been lost in transit).

Do I think Karl Wallenda was afraid of walking that tightrope without a safety net? Sure I do. But there were things that drove Wallenda that made him what he was in his day—an entrepreneur. He was willing to walk out into the unknown, take risks that few others were willing to take, all in the hopes of being his own man, running his own life, and building something that might last for generations.

Karl Wallenda was a brilliant man and a superstar among tightrope walkers.

My father, likewise, was a brilliant man—a superstar when it came to his skillset and work. He had the endurance to stand pain and sweat and work, and he could push a project to the end; but if he didn't get a check on Friday and work *for* somebody, it scared him to death.

My father always wanted to own his own business. But at the end of the day, he couldn't bring himself to do it. He just couldn't. There are some people that can walk out there on that wire, and if there is a net under them, man, they can walk and dance on that tightrope. But you pull that net away with nothing but an abyss underneath them, and they're not going out on that wire, no matter how much money might be on the other side. They'll tell you right quick, "You want somebody to go? Go yourself."

Facing Down Fear

Not that long ago, I read an account of Nik Wallenda's (Karl's grandson) walk between the Chicago Towers. The article said that Wallenda wasn't scared because he was prepared for what was ahead. My first thought was, "That guy was lying for the press." I don't know a single person in business for himself who doesn't get a punch in the gut of fear before he walks out on the wire. Maybe not every day, maybe not regularly, but before a man takes that first step into a big risky situation, you can bet one thing: he feels that fear.

When you feel that gut-wrenching fear in the pit of your stomach, that's how you know you're going to fight to succeed. For some of us, that feeling is a drug we're hooked on until our dying days. There is nothing in this world that stimulates my senses like the insurmountable challenges of starting and running a business. Your mental and physical toughness will be tested on a daily basis.

People believe that when you reach a certain point in business, you can rest, breathe deeply, and relax. When the day comes that you *want* to rest and breathe, you need to cash in your chips and go sit in the cheap seats with the spectators.

Have I ever gotten scared? I don't think you'll ever be in business long enough that it won't be scary. I get so scared sometimes I can't tell you my name. I have anxiety and doubt and everything that goes with it, but I have faith in two things: God and myself. If you stay out of my way and leave me out on the tightrope long enough, I will absolutely get to the other side.

If a guy tells me, "Oh, it's just another deal. We'll make some good money. It's practically a sure thing." He's lying. He's hiding something, and I won't do the deal with him. If a guy tells me there's no fear in the back of his mind, he's lying. If a guy tells you he climbed Everest, and he's not afraid of heights, that guy's a liar. You don't hang off of pegs 3,000 feet above the ground and not feel fear. It makes no difference how many times you walk out on the wire—you're going to feel that prick of fear. But you have to push through it. You always have to push through, whether it's life or business. You have to have an iron will and say, "I will succeed. I will push through this," and it will happen.

When I first went into business, I struggled during the hard times. I worried if I'd be able to pay my bills. I worried if my wife would get fed up and leave me. I worried about a lot of things, some of which happened, but many of which didn't (don't worry, my wife's still with me). But over time, I have come to recognize the fear as part of the process, part of what drives me and makes me successful. I have become acclimated to the fear and accept it as necessary and beneficial.

WALKING THE TIGHTROPE

I had a soldier tell me once that armies suffer a higher casualty rate when they first experience combat situations. But the longer that company is in combat, the lower their casualty rate is because they acclimate to the situation and acquire the skills necessary to increase their chances for survival. They become acclimated to the fear and they overcome it.

Karl Wallenda overcame a significant obstacle when he and his hand-selected, hand-trained team walked into Madison Square Garden. He had worked hard to get to the level of having a ring at The Ringling Brother's Circus, and you can bet he wasn't going to let something as simple as a missing net keep him from achieving his goals. He faced down his fear and created a business that spanned generations.

In your business, you are going to come up against some obstacles that will feel insurmountable; you will have to battle fatigue, fear, and failure constantly, and you'll have to fight to get your foot in the door.

You have to remember that these are obstacles, not impossibilities. You can overcome them. You can go around them, climb over them, or plow through them. You just have to believe that you can. You have to make a plan and viciously and diligently execute it.

Perception versus Reality

One of the biggest lessons I learned in business was how to get people to take me seriously. It started with getting my dad to take me seriously when I was a teenager wanting to start my own business. From there, as a young twenty-something, I had to get people to take me seriously, just like I did with the Missouri Pacific Railroad. And the way I got them to take me seriously was I presented an image of myself that led them to perceive me a certain way.

Perception is reality because when it comes to business, people will believe what they perceive. If they think you are an expert in your field, they will treat you like one. If they perceive you are a lazy bum looking to make a quick buck, they'll treat you like that too.

I once knew a kid named Johnny—a smart kid trying to make it. I was sitting in the bank when Johnny came in one day. He walked through the bank with a pair of dirty pants on, dirty boots, an old t-shirt, and three days' worth of beard on his face. He was in there to borrow some money and was trying to talk to one of the bank's lending officers. I asked the bank president, "How long y'all been doing business with Johnny?"

The banker looked at me like I was an idiot, and said, "We don't do business with Johnny now, and we aren't going to do any business with Johnny in the future." I laughed and said, "Really, why not? That kid's smart." He looked back out at Johnny, shrugged his shoulders and said, "You know something? That kid just looks like a bum to me."

The thing is, that kid was smart and a really hard worker. He just didn't look the part, so the banker believed what he perceived to be the truth. And his perception of Johnny kept him from giving Johnny the resources he needed to make a go of his business.

Seems like a common sense thing to me, but it bears repeating because I've seen too many guys forget this. **If you want to be in business, look like you're in business.** People should see you working hard to be a good guy- involved in your community, working hard, donating your time and your money.

If you are going to survive and be successful, you have to play the game every day. When you walk out of your house, you have to have a haircut and your fingernails need to be clean. If you want people to treat you like you're somebody, then you better look like you're somebody. You better walk like you're somebody and talk like you're somebody.

When General Patton assumed command of the Third Army during World War II; His larger than life personality transformed an army, with no combat experience, into the most celebrated combat army of World War II. His unyielding discipline was legendary, especially toward his staff and officers. He demanded that they dress and conduct themselves as leaders at all times.

General Patton wanted his staff to present themselves to the troops as *leaders.* The more they dressed like leaders, the more they acted like leaders, and the more they were perceived as leaders. Maybe it seems old school to some of you in this day where everything is more casual. But let me make my point one more time, people will treat you like the person and business they think you are. Dress the part. If you want to be taken seriously, dress the part.

Be Persistent

When you start off in business, you might not have all the training and resources you need to do the job. To that I say, "So what?" You don't have to know it all to get started. But you do have to get prepared for the life of a business owner, and you have to be persistent in working toward what you want to achieve, no matter how big the obstacles feel.

Think of it this way, how long does it take a kid to learn to walk? How long does it take a kid to learn to run? How long does it take that kid to learn to be a world-class athlete and go to the Olympics? It takes a whole lot of time and a whole lot of practice, and it includes falling flat on your face from time to time.

I think one of the most shocking revelations for new business owners is how often they feel beaten down. The fact is they are going to get beaten down for a good number of years before they get to the top of their game. It's like being a world champion boxer in your weight division. You have to like the beating or you can't enjoy the victory. You have to prepare yourself for the fact that you are going to get punched in the face every time you step in the ring. As a business owner, you're going to get beat up, you're going to get run over, and you're going to get hammered. If you want to keep running your business, you'll need to learn to love the challenge and the pain.

People often ask me for the steps to starting a business. They want to know what it takes to be successful. But when I sit down and start talking about things like perception and persistence they say, "No. What *steps* do I need to take?" But you know, different guys take different paths. Every business is different; every deal in every business is different. If someone tells you there is an A plus B equals C formula to starting and running a successful business, they are blowing smoke up your skirt.

Like I said in your Chapter Three Take Away, when you make the decision to own your own company, you can control two things, and only two things. You can control how you start and how you finish.

How do you control the start?

Do your research and build a concise business plan.

How do you control the finish?

Set goals and stay laser-focused on your business plan.

In between the start and the finish, what's it going to take you to get there? Who knows? You need to understand the beginning and understand what the goal is. Once you start, don't ever look back at the beginning, and just look straight ahead at the goal.

Think of running your business like playing middle linebacker. You get out there on that field, and you're going to have the opportunity to run over a lot of people, but if you stay on that field long enough, they're going to hit you back and hit you hard. If you can't get up, spit your teeth out, wipe the blood off, and go back in there and shoot for the goal, then don't get in the game.

Fighting the Big Companies

And lastly, if you're willing to get in the game, and you're prepared to persevere through the obstacles, then you need to be ready to fight for every inch of the market you can get.

In every market there's an entry point. There's a niche to

exploit somewhere in that market. There are people who control a certain amount of that market, who have been in it a long time, who have all the connections, and can call in all the favors in the world. If you go head-to-head with those guys, you're going to go down in flames before you even get off the ground.

You've got to understand that you may be going up against a guy that's got 20 years of experience. When you get up against that guy, you'll almost always come in second. It's not because you don't have money or resources. That guy is a skilled infighter. He knows the tricks of the trade. It's those guys you have to fight through to make it in business. But if you use your head and constantly look at new ways to enter the market, you just might come out on top.

A perfect example is Herbert "Herb" Kelleher, the founder of Southwest Airlines. Herb wanted to start an airline that was cheap and didn't have all the frills or the overhead that the big guns had, and he wanted to fly only in Texas. Their slogan was, "Long legs and short nights," a unique market entry that took big name airline companies completely by surprise! Who can forget those skimpy uniforms and white go-go boots? Initially, when Kelleher was up against Continental and three other (now defunct) airlines, they crushed him at every turn. They owned the lobbies and got every law and injunction passed that it took to keep him out of their hangars. They hammered him from daylight to dark, but he didn't go away. He kept at it. Now Southwest Airlines is one of the top airlines in the nation and has the highest number of return customers overall.

Another great example is George Washington and the colonial army. While fighting the British in the Colonial War, George Washington quickly figured out that in a head-to-head shootout with the British, his men would come out second because the British Army knew how to stay in rank and file, deliver a volley, and hit the bull's-eye. He knew the Colonial Army would suffer horrendous losses because the other guys were better trained in that kind of fighting. So they beat the British by coming at them with a different game plan. They used a type of guerilla warfare tactic that brought the British to their knees.

Big companies (and big armies) aren't scared of the fight. They'll spend money and battle and push until they get what they want. You have to think like a creator when you go up against the companies with the biggest market share. And remember this, nobody gets 100 percent of the market. It never happens. There are always a group of disenfranchised customers in a freemarket system. There are always some guys that say, "You know what? Microsoft is the best deal in the world, but I just don't like Bill Gates. He's just a goofball that combs his hair wrong. So, I'm going to buy something else." That's your niche. Your business can swoop down and say, "Okay, let's go get as much of those disenfranchised guys as we can. Let's take care of them. Let's treat them like kings, even though they're the little guys." When you do that, you start building that base and before you know it, you're taking on empires.

Once you've got that company fleshed out and you're getting your bills paid, you can turn your attention to the big guy. You can start a guerilla war with him that he won't win.

When I started my aggregate business in Houston, there was a very influential family that controlled the aggregate business in most of the city and surrounding area. To say they were entrenched is like calling the Mississippi River a creek. They were connected in every way imaginable from the tip-top to the very bottom of politics. They did their homework, kept their name clean, and took care of business; they marched in lock step. When you walked around them, you sensed they were an awesome machine, one that worked with precision.

Upon first look they were a German Panzer tank striking fear and admiration in all that faced them. But like all companies, the Panzer had its Achilles heel also. The Panzer could withstand brutal punishment from three sides; the front and both sides, but one well-placed shot to the rear, and the tank was out of commission. My goal with my competition was to figure out where their soft underbelly lay, like the Panzer. The trick with them was also the same as the Panzer. It's wasn't the size of the shot or how many, it was simply placing that one shot in the correct place that would turn the battle. And like the Panzer, I also had to get by that terrible noise they created. Everywhere I went around Houston I heard the same sermon. "You go up against those guys, and they'll wear you out. Nobody sells aggregate in Houston but them."

When you're looking at a market, it's the same as looking at your enemies' territory. The first step is to know his territory and him better than he knows either one. I had done just that with the market on the east side of Houston. The first thing I did was to fly over the area to understand the rail system, the distance of the nearest aggregate suppliers, and product demand, both present and long term. The second thing I did was to understand how my competition was owned and managed. The management of their company was all second and third-generation family. They had all the perks in life that generational wealth brings and that was their Achilles heel. When people have that kind of wealth, their primary focus often becomes spending money, not making money.

When a company reaches a certain point in its growth, it's better managed by a group of trained professionals who will focus and react to market conditions and not their lifestyle. If their management and market conditions had been different, I would have applied a completely different tactic. But their lifestyle was making their company rigid and non-responsive to their customer's needs. This was the message that was being whispered behind their back by their customers and employees alike.

My tactic was half Walmart and half Mercedes Benz. The Walmart half was that we were open seven days a week, twenty-four hours a day. My competitor opened at seven in the morning and closed promptly at 4:30, and it didn't matter how good of a customer you were. There was no give to the policy. The Mercedes Benz half of the strategy was price and dependability. We weren't the cheapest but we worked around the clock in all kinds of weather, and when the phone rang we answered it. We became the Special Forces in our market; if you wanted it done right and on time with a 110% guaranteed success rate, you called us.

It was a level of competitiveness that our competitor couldn't match and didn't care to. So we began to get more and more of their business.

We cut our part of the market out and pretty soon had our arms around what we wanted. That became our focus and our lifestyle. There is always a way in, but you've got to be creative to get what you want. And more than anything else, no matter what comes at you, you have to face your fears and step out on that tightrope, over and over and over again.

Action Steps:

In this chapter, I said you could control two things: how you start and how you finish (crossing the goal line).

When you answer the following questions, you will have a plan on how to start.

- What do you need to get started?

- Who is your competition?

- How big is the market?

- What will your niche be?

- What will make you unique? Will it be price, product, or location?

The Take Away:

Don't let fear keep you from succeeding. Use your fear to fuel your passion and get you to the finish line. Running your business is like being a Navy Seal. The day you stop craving the action, get out!

CHAPTER SIX

KEEPING YOUR INTEGRITY

"It's infinitely better to walk away from a dishonest deal with your integrity than with a briefcase full of money. You might not eat as well for a while, but you'll sure sleep better."

— Robert S. Lott

It started with a lucky rabbit named Oswald, not with a mouse. Walt Disney created Oswald the Lucky Rabbit in 1927, with his chief animator, Ub Iwerks. Oswald was an animated success; not only did he draw praise from the press, but Oswald merchandise flew off shelves. The animated rabbit with personality set the new standard for cartoons and allowed Disney's fledgling studio to thrive.

But Oswald the Lucky Rabbit would prove to be not-so-lucky for Disney. In 1928, Charles Mintz, Disney's distributor, convinced some of Disney's animators to leave and work with him in a new studio. At the same time, Universal informed Disney it owned the rights to Oswald. In one swift motion, Disney lost it all. Unprotected in any way by a contract, young entrepreneur Disney was left with virtually nothing.

But as with most entrepreneurs, Disney's defeat fueled his desire to pick himself up and start over. On the train ride home, after learning he'd lost it all, Disney created Mickey Mouse - and the rest is history. Oswald was finally able to join the ranks of Disney's household animated names in 2006, when the company reacquired the rights.

While the suffering and living on the edge of poverty may feed the soul of a true entrepreneur, there's a magical process of evolution when a business begins to unfold and come to life. Something is created that few people will ever get the chance to experience. Walt Disney knew that magical process, and he pursued it.

Survival at All Costs

In business, some will say it makes no difference how you get there as long as you survive the process. I harshly disagree! When I was trying to get my first business started, a very successful business owner told me that the first and last rule of business was survival. I will never forget the look in his eyes as he spoke the word survival. There was a darkness I saw there in his eyes, the depth of which I knew a person could not escape if ever once they traveled there. There was no doubt in my mind he would do whatever it took to stay in business—whatever it took. I truly believe he would have sold his soul to the devil if that's what it took to keep his business afloat.

That statement has served me well all of my life, but perhaps not in the way he thought it would. I made the decision then and there that there were two things I would never sacrifice just to survive: my family, and my integrity.

It's easy to find yourself in a place of having to make compromising decisions in business. You have to make the moral decision every single day to make the right choice, to choose the right way. And don't mistake the easy way as being the right way. It rarely is. Decide early on what you will and won't sacrifice to succeed. Write it down somewhere and refer back to it if you need it.

I knew I WOULD be willing to sacrifice:

- **My finances** – In the beginning, my goals were just to be able to pay my bills. I wasn't looking to get rich quick. I knew my finances were going to take a hit (maybe many times) but it was a sacrifice I was willing to make.

- **My friendships** – You go ahead and judge me if you want to about this, but I knew that if it came down to my friends or my business, I'd walk away from friendships in order to build a business that would help me reach my goals. You're going to have to sacrifice something to succeed, so when you make your list, you better make an honest one.

- **My personal time** – I said I wouldn't sacrifice my family, meaning I wouldn't get so focused on building a successful business that I would run my wife and kids into the ground. But I did decide that I would be willing to sacrifice some of my personal time, and that sometimes meant time with my family.

- **My relationships with people who lacked integrity** – It's a hard thing to walk away from a business deal that involves a lot of money. But the first time you decide to do some shady deal with a guy or a company, just because you don't want to lose the contact or the possible deals that guy's going to bring your way . . . well, let me just say it this way, "You sell your soul to the devil just one time for money, you do it over and over and over." I made the decision early on that

I would not do business with people who lacked integrity, even if I had to sever the relationship permanently.

If you operate with a mindset of "survival at all costs," you might make a whole lot of money, but you'll end up with nothing of value in your life.

Trust, but Verify

During the Geneva Summit of 1985 and 1988, Ronald Reagan realized that the US was going to have to "do business" with Russia if they had a shot at ending the Cold War. During those summits and at the signing of the Arms Treaty, Reagan repeated an Old Russian proverb which translated into, "Trust, but verify." He knew he would have to trust the information he was getting from Soviet President Mikhail Gorbachev. But he also knew he needed to be smart and verify the information.

After many years of deciding exactly how they would reduce the nuclear armament of both countries, the men shook hands, and then they followed up their agreement with a written contract, the Strategic Arms Reduction Treaty of 1991.

Sometimes, you're going to have to do business with an evil empire. That is a fact, no matter what your business is.

And there will be instances where you will do business on a handshake, but if that happens you better know whose hand you're shaking, and you better follow it up with something in writing. And as a side note, don't make handshake deals standard operating practice in your day-to-day business.

Business is a competitive sport that is governed by contracts or client guidelines. Even where there are contracts and long-standing relationships, money has the ability to transform people into the worst version of themselves. Money can turn a moral compass due south in a hurry. And sadly, some people are just looking for an opportunity to beat you out of your money.

I saw firsthand one of my competitors lose a 10-million-dollar-per-year client over a clause in their contract with a typo. The owner of the contracting company enforced the contract according to the typo, which resulted in his client's invoice being $80,000 instead of $8,000. The client tried every way in the world to negotiate the $80,000 down to something reasonable, but the contractor refused. In his own eyes, the contractor was in the right, and he meant to collect. The client eventually wrote the check, but it was followed by an interoffice memo removing the contractor from all future bid lists.

The contractor, aware of his lack of integrity on the deal, continued to call the senior VPs to inquire as to why his sales calls weren't being returned. The VP politely informed the contractor they had all of the approved contractors needed at the time. Many years later, the contractor had still never been reinstated. The stories in business that will follow you around the longest are the ones where you sacrifice your integrity for the sake of a dollar.

The real aftermath comes from the word of mouth from your competitors. Trust me, you'll encounter plenty of business disasters naturally without the unnecessary interference of a tarnished reputation following you around.

And when money is involved without a contract in place, people will lose their integrity quicker than lightning can strike. You can count on it.

Be smart about the deals you make, with whom you make them, and how you go about making them. Don't let money and power influence your decision-making skills. You'll never come out on top.

You Can Call A Leopard By Any Name You Want To But It's Still A Leopard

Your integrity is one of the most important assets you own in business because it is the foundation of your reputation. You shouldn't manipulate people to get ahead. I will put myself out there to make deals, and I will work hard and fast to make them happen, but working hard and fast is not manipulating. You can make money and lose money on any one business, but if you're honest and do the right thing, people will help you get started again. If you run your business with integrity, your reputation will allow for new options and opportunities to arise.

I have a very smart friend who used to make money like you wouldn't believe. I'll tell you though, I never did any kind of deal with him. He would hammer you at his first opportunity and beat you out of every dollar you had coming without batting an eye. When the deal started making money, he just couldn't help himself. Money was his mistress and there was no shame too great or small that he wouldn't endure to come out on top. He has and always will have the DNA of a crook, it's just that plain and simple.

Now he's at an age in life when everybody in the business community knows he's a crook. Every job he ever managed made money, but his stealing and dishonest record keeping always caught up to him. There isn't anyone now that would dare risk their reputation to be associated with him. Even though he is blessed with all the great attributes of a brilliant businessman and leader, he struggles just to make a living in the construction industry. He is a pariah and everyone knows it.

You can call a leopard by any name you want to, but he's still a leopard. He'll still bite you, no matter what. Once people get to know you for what you are, there's very little you can do to change their minds. Integrity and reputation are inseparable.

Way back in the beginning, when I convinced that equipment guy to give me that equipment for little more than a promise, I gave the guy his rock. I did what I said I would do. I had a feeling I would need his help again along the way. Sure enough, he let me have some equipment further down the road when my money was tight and I couldn't pay him. When you tell someone you're going to do something, you better get it done.

This is true when deals get hard or start going wrong for reasons out of your control. You can't just up and walk away like you're purely a spectator. You have to hold on until the bones are breaking and the blood is flying. **Because the true test of character is how well you stand in there and manage when everything is headed straight for disaster.**

If you suffer a failure, and you will sooner or later because no one has or ever will have a perfect scorecard, even if you lose money, the fact that you stayed in the game and worked your guts out to lessen the disaster will speak volumes about your integrity. People always watch how you react when the chips are down.

And, if you stay in business long enough, you will eventually experience a situation where you hold all of the aces. It's rare, but it happens. In that scenario, you will have a chance to set yourself apart from your competitors by being fair when the contract says different.

The best business decisions are the ones that reveal your integrity. If you succeed because you walked on people to make a dollar, then the victories will always be hollow. I would rather fail a hundred times over than know what I have acquired in life was through any other means than honest work.

Action Steps:

1. In Chapter One, you took an honest look at yourself, your reasons for going into business, and what you would be willing to sacrifice to build and grow a successful business. Pull that list out.

2. Now make a list of the things you won't sacrifice.

3. Put both lists where you can easily find them on hard days and during hard times.

The Take Away:

Survival at all cost always comes with a price that you'll never like paying.

CHAPTER SEVEN

WHO IS GETTING ON THE BUS?

"If you, the bus driver (business owner), aren't careful about how you fill the seats on your bus, you'll drive your business around in circles."

— Robert S. Lott

Jim Collins, author of "Good to Great," equated the operation of a business to a ride on a bus.

Collins wrote,

You are a bus driver. The bus, your company, is at a standstill, and it's your job to get it going. You have to decide where you're going, how you're going to get there, and who's going with you.

Most people assume that great bus drivers (read: business leaders) immediately start the journey by announcing to the people on the bus where they're going—by setting a new direction or by articulating a fresh corporate vision.

In fact, leaders of companies that go from good to great start not with "where" but with "who." They start by getting the right people on the bus, the wrong people off the bus, and the right people in the right seats. And they stick with that discipline—first the people, then the direction—no matter what.[2]

There is a fine art to finding and hiring the right people for your business, any business, really, large or small. But the task is increasingly more difficult when it comes to hiring people for your small business. Initially, you aren't going to have the money, the benefits, and all the attractive perks that big companies have to attract quality employees.

---

2. Collins, Jim. "Good to Great." Jim Collins. October 1, 2001. Accessed February 9, 2015. http://www.jimcollins.com/article_topics/articles/good-to-great.html.

WHO IS GETTING ON THE BUS?

You've got two things that will be attractive to someone who is a high-caliber hire: your passion for your business and a laser focus on how to get to your goals. Driven people want to work for driven people. So don't think for a second you can't get high-caliber employees to come to work for you, because you can.

You do have to have a plan though. When you are thinking through the details of your business, think about all the possible hires you will want to make over the years and then develop a strategy for who you want to hire, where you will find them, and how they can be moved to different seats on the bus as the company grows. For example, when I first started out, I would go around to other companies to find a guy that was pretty good at his job, but stuck in a position with no shot at moving up or making more money. Guys like that know they don't have any opportunity where they are, and can see the benefit of striking out with a fairly new company where they might have the chance of moving up some day.

Take care of guys like that. You can also find a few already working or hire them right out of college when they're still used to eating Ramen noodles every day. You'll be able to pay them $40,000 a year or something you can afford. That's an entry-level job for them, and they may stay with you for a couple of years. When they gain new skill sets and experience, they may go somewhere else. Or, they may grow with the company and you may decide to keep them. Either way, having good people on the bus, even if it's just for a short while, can do wonders for growing your business.

Finding the Right Fit

I interviewed a gifted guy from a big company who, for whatever reason, wanted to make a change. He had an MBA from Harvard, and I was looking for a CFO. The company was kind of small for what this guy had been doing, and I could tell right off he was going to struggle. Compared to the employees from his old job, where they all had a college degree and most had a master's, he was going to have to deal with my company where most of the girls working in my office didn't even have college degrees.

I could tell that even though he was a brilliant guy who could add value to my organization, at the end of the day he wasn't going to become a functional piece of the business. He was going to have to learn to run a company with a smaller budget and fewer people and resources than he was used to, and I didn't think he would survive. People called me crazy for not hiring him, but he wasn't the right person for the job. A great person, yes, just not great for the position.

WHO IS GETTING ON THE BUS?

Hiring the wrong person for the job can do more damage than running lean for the short term, while you're looking for the right guy. I don't mean hire someone who acts and thinks just like I do. That's not what I mean by the "right" guy. Personally, when I hire someone, I don't really care what they do on their own time. I don't care what they like or don't like, what their politics are, what god they worship, if they're gay or straight. None of that matters to me. When I hire someone, this is what I care about: can they pull the cleats tight, put the helmet on, and go play to win? After they leave work, they can go be anything they want to be.

However, the person you hire does have to fit the culture of your business. For example, there was an engineer who wanted to work for me, but I would never hire him. Not because he wasn't smart, and not because he couldn't have done some amazing work for me. The problem was the guy was a jerk. His IQ was off the chart, so he pretty much talked down to most people and struggled to communicate with them. In my business, if you go in the room and your goal is to make sure that everybody knows you're the smartest guy in the room, then you won't make it on my team. We don't act like that in my company. Everyone has a job, everyone pulls his weight, and everyone works hard all day long. No one is smarter or better or more important than anyone else. I don't hand important responsibilities and big paychecks to someone who isn't willing to push themselves, all day, every day. On this team, we are all high performers.

Family and Money

Owning your own business often adds an interesting element to family dynamics. A lot of your family will want to get on the bus. Trust me on this. They not only want to get on the bus, they feel entitled to the best seat on the bus. And if you, the bus driver (business owner), aren't careful about how you fill the seats on your bus, you'll drive your business around in circles.

It may sound harsh, but your friends and your family rarely help you build a company, and smart guys that own companies usually put those people at the back of the line. Don't get me wrong. I have hired my family members to work in my business from time to time. In fact, at different times and for different reasons, I hired both my son and my daughter. But when I hired them, my expectations weren't that they would work as hard as everyone else on my payroll. My expectations were that they would work *harder* than everyone else.

When my son graduated from college, he couldn't find a job and came to work for me. I didn't mind helping him, but you can bet that in return for a job and a paycheck, I expected a full day's work out of him. But he'd lived that college lifestyle for a number of years and was having a hard time making the adjustment to the real world. He wasn't used to getting up at 6:00 in the morning and working until 6:00 in the evening. Eventually, I sat him down and said, "I'm going to tell you what I'm going to do with you. I'm going to save you and me both a lot of embarrassment. You go find you a job, or I'm going to fire you; take your pick. You're not going to come to work when you want to and do what you want to around here. No one is on the bench in this company. I demand others work all day long, and I do that myself. Everybody is in the game, playing the full length of the game clock. You either play at that level and step up because you draw a check like they do, or you're out."

He had graduated from The University of Texas at Austin with a great education and with all the talent in the world. He just didn't know how to use it yet, and he would have never learned how working for me, because his survival didn't depend on it. He needed to be in an environment where he knew there was no one to save him from being eaten except himself. Sometimes hiring your family, regardless of your intentions, is just not the best thing for everyone concerned.

My son went off and found himself a job on his own, and after two hard years, he learned to use his education and grew up by a quantum leap. He returned to my organization and became a stand out performer helping me through some very tough times. He has since moved on to a publicly-traded company where he is rising through the ranks with the work ethic of a high performer.

On the other side of the coin, my daughter came to me and wanted to run my safety department. She was an English teacher and a great writer, and the safety department is mainly about writing policy. When she asked for the job, I said, "I'm going to tell you straight up, you're not tough enough. I love you, but you're not tough enough. I work the people in that department like pack mules because I have a good safety record, and I'm going to keep it. Whoever is in there is going to go above and beyond to take care of the people in the field. You're a school teacher; you're used to being off and having set hours—you won't do it." I misjudged that girl by a million miles.

One day she called and said, "I quit my job teaching school. I just can't do it. I resigned. I want to go to work for you."

So I sat her down and said, "Okay. Go buy yourself a pair of lace-up boots, buy some Nomex, (which is fire retardant clothing), get a hard hat and safety glasses, and you go to the field. Be there at 5:00 when they start in the morning, and watch them tie in pipe. Learn everything my people do. You do that, then I'll bring you in and let you work in the safety department."

I said, "If you're late and you don't do it, I'm going to run you off. I'll let you go find a job, or I'll fire you in front of God and everybody else."

She started work and to my disbelief she was in the field day and night. She became involved in every aspect of construction safety until she knew the business forwards and backwards. After several years of rising through the ranks she ultimately became the head of my safety department. Under her leadership our safety record became the gold standard in the pipeline construction industry. In 2010, she left my company and started her own safety company, which has a clientele of the who's who in the midstream construction industry.

My employees are high performers, whether they are family or friends, or some Joe I hired off the street. If you become an underperformer in my company, no matter who you are, you're going out the door pretty quick.

Companies go broke every day by letting family and friends have jobs instead of hiring the right people. You get a reputation for only hiring family and friends, then the extremely talented graduates will say, "Nah, I'm not going to work there because he puts more value on family and friends than he does on performance." And they don't come to work for you.

At the end of the day, my point is this: Who you let on the bus with you will determine the success (or failure) of your company. No one should get on that bus just because they are related to you or have a relationship with you. They should get a seat on the bus only if they are qualified for the job. Period.

Kick 'em off the Bus

A chapter on who to hire wouldn't be complete without including how to fire someone when you've made a bad hiring decision. The only person who has any control of who gets on and stays on the bus is the bus driver, you, the business owner. Inevitably, the problems that come from making the wrong hiring decision surface and you have no one to blame but yourself. There's only one thing you can do when you've let someone on your bus that doesn't belong there. You've got to kick 'em off the bus.

Bill Hybels, founder of the Leadership Summit, said in his speech at the 2013 Summit,

When it comes to letting someone go, I use a 30 day system. If they are not performing well, I'll give them 90 days to make a plan to change and prove to me they can. If they have personal problems that are affecting their job, I'll give them 60 days to get the

help they need and prove to me they still belong on the bus. If they have a bad attitude, I'll give them 30 days to fix it, and then I'll tell them, 'I'm not firing you. I'm firing your bad attitude.'[3]

He's dead on. If someone's working hard, but they just aren't doing their jobs right, I'll give them a little bit of time to get their game up to speed and prove to me they can still be a valuable player before I'll let them go. If someone's personal life is wreaking havoc on their job performance, I'll give them some time to get their head in the game before I'll fire them. And in both of those cases, if someone has to be let go, I do it with dignity. But if someone has a bad attitude about me, my customers, my business, or other employees, I don't give them much time at all. A bad attitude in a business is like a cancer. Unless you treat it quickly and decisively, it will spread. If someone can't be a team player, you can bet they're getting kicked off the bus without even slowing down.

---

3. Hybels, Bill. "From Bill Hybels." The Global Leadership Summit. Accessed February 9, 2015. https://www.willowcreek. com/events/leadership/from_bill_hybels_rsp.asp.

Action Steps:

1. Write out a hiring guideline that will be used to fill every position in your company. This guideline is invaluable when your friends and family begin to ask for (or demand) a job.

2. Write out a second guideline on how you will go about recruiting the right people to fill the positions.

3. Then ask yourself these questions:

   - When do you see yourself hiring your first employee?

   - What skill sets will they need?

   - Where will you find these people?

The Take Away:

As friends and family get on the bus, talent gets off the bus. Hire the right people for the job.

CHAPTER EIGHT

PASSION WON'T PAY
THE BILLS

"You can have an idea for your business and a burning desire to succeed, but if you can't sell your product, you're left with just a great idea and a lot of passion. And that doesn't pay the bills."

— Robert S. Lott

Kirby vacuums were invented when another household appliance giant, Hoover, was already flourishing. The creators of the Kirby vacuum thought they had a product that could compete with the already popular Hoover. The Kirby line of vacuums took the idea of cleaning to the next level and introduced removable floor nozzles and handles. Over time they refined the product, and it has now been in homes for over 100 years.

But that wasn't all Kirby did. They knew their vacuum had to stand apart from the other brands being sold in the stores, and they chose to sell it through direct sales only. In 1920, the company began selling their vacuums door-to-door so customers could experience the Kirby difference firsthand. They also sold them at a higher price and marketed them to housewives as the luxury in vacuum cleaners.

Of course, there were naysayers who told the folks at Kirby they were doing it all wrong. But the proof is in the sales record, and all these years later, Kirby vacuums can still only be purchased through direct sales. They are also still considered the luxury brand of vacuum cleaners.

You can have an idea for your business and a burning desire to succeed, but if you can't sell your product, you're left with just a great idea and a lot of passion. And that doesn't pay the bills.

The Three Questions You Have To Ask

The people over at Kirby had lots of decisions to make when it came to how they would sell their product. But they held true to their notion that they had the best vacuum on the market, despite the fact that their competition, Hoover, was almost synonymous with the word vacuum. But Kirby believed in their product and they had a desire to sell vacuums differently.

Kirby asked themselves three primary questions, and they are the same three questions you'll have to ask yourself, too:

1. What am I selling?
2. Who am I selling to?
3. How is it different than my competition?

Answering these questions will save you a lot of time and hassle down the road. As you train your sales force, there will be a clear vision for what it is you are selling, who you are selling to, and what your competitive advantage in the market is. If you just start selling your product without an understanding of exactly what it is you're selling, you're going to find yourself out of money before the company even has a real chance to get going.

Kirby vacuums understood they were selling a vacuum, like many other companies, but they refined it over the years to make it easier to use and with more features. They knew their target market was the housewife who prided herself on having a clean home for her family. And Kirby knew they were different because they came directly into your home to show you how their product worked. They also marketed their product as a luxury vacuum so clients who purchased it felt a sense of superiority over others who purchased just another vacuum at the store.

Your ability to survive as a business will depend on how you answer those three questions. Your answers will be the headlights for your business along your journey.

Know Your Product

Your product should have a clear and concise definition of what it does. It has to be as clear as looking at a bull's-eye from three feet away. You'll need to completely wrap yourself in what your product is and how it works; understand how it is made and what the benefits of it are. You should know the product like the back of your hand, because if you don't, people you are trying to sell to will see right through you.

When I was sitting in the lobby of the Missouri Pacific Office Building five days a week waiting to see someone about leasing those four acres of land, I knew what my product was going to be. I knew I had something special in those four acres, and I was able to convince the railroad and the equipment rental guy that what I had was worth it.

It didn't matter how old I was at the time. It didn't matter how much money I did or didn't have. It mattered that I knew what my product was, and everyone I spoke to about it knew without a doubt I was going to make good on making that product a success. After all these years of starting businesses, one of the first things I do is make sure I know my product better than anyone else.

Know Your Market

It's not enough to just know your product inside and out. At the end of the day, your customers are going to be the ones writing your paychecks, so it's important to know who those customers will be. Your target market will be the specific market segment that your company is going to sell your product to. Knowing your target market isn't just the first part of a good sales strategy; it's also the first part of a good marketing strategy.

Hone in on your target market and get to know them - understand their buying behaviors, the way the competition does business with them, and what the future for your product looks like through their eyes. You need to know specifically who your customers are going to be. What are their needs? What do they want? How do they want it presented to them?

Make sure your target market is well-defined and not too general. For example, if you have a men's clothing store you can't just say your target market is men. What type of man? What industry does this man work in? What is his income level? And for the love of Moses, do not say your target market is everyone. If that's your answer, you need to rework some of your strategy because no business is ever able to successfully reach a target market as broad as "everyone."

A few helpful questions to ask as you develop your target market are:

- Am I trying to reach males, females or both?
- What is the age bracket of my target market?
- Where does my target market live?
- What is the income of my target market?
- What is the education level of my target market?
- Where do they get information?
- What are common objections to my product?
- Who are my competitors targeting?

Of course, these aren't all the questions you'll ask as you start to develop your target market, but they are a good place to get started. There are companies out there that can help you further research your target market as it gets more defined. Doing your homework on whom you're selling to is a crucial step in sales success.

Know Why You're Different

If you had enough passion to start a company, you should easily know why your product is different from the rest. What makes you different should also begin to re-define who your target market is, which then creates a niche market. Remember how I found clients in an already saturated aggregate market? I honed in on an area of land that wasn't already reached, and I set myself apart from my competition by being available 24/7.

Understanding why you're different from the competition is the same thing as fighting a battle. Remember the story about George Washington and his colonial army? Washington recognized that both sides were fighting a battle and at the end of the day, someone would have to be the victor. But Washington found his own angle. He used guerilla warfare the British hadn't seen before and because of that, they couldn't defeat Washington's army. He changed the course of history because he had enough guts to find an angle that wasn't being used, and he found what he needed to win. He found his competitive advantage.

But Washington couldn't have come up with his guerilla warfare tactic without first knowing what the British were doing. I've stated this many times before: one of the main keys to success is knowing your competition. You have to study their market strategy and know from day one what makes them click. When you've committed your market tactics to memory, then it's time to act. The next step is to gather the resources that will sustain your plan of action. If your resources can't support your strategy, then you need to reevaluate your plan of action. Some battles can be fought with limited resources and some can't. The point I am making here is pick your battles very carefully. Remember you can control the outcome to your benefit, but you must be realistic. If you spend enough time with something like Washington did, you'll begin to see a path forward to success that fits your resources and talents. Never let your ego dictate the course of the fight. Your ego is sustained by success and it is better to feed it many small successes than gamble on one huge winner-take-all fight. Also, like in Washington's case, enough small victories will lead to winning the war, and that is the ultimate goal.

It's Still Not the Size of the Dog

When you know your product inside and out, when you know the target market that you want to sell to, and when you have a firm grasp of what makes you different, then it's time to get out there and get your feet wet. And remember, some of your competition will be bigger. And meaner. But remember, it isn't the size of the dog, it's the size of the fight in the dog. So be a pit bull!

Lots of the companies I started had competitors that were bigger and seemed fiercer. There were times when I could easily have let myself be intimidated and backed out, but I refused. If I had the right resources in hand, and I knew I had something that was better than what the rest of the competition had, I was going to stick it out and be relentless. I already told you, I worked lots of hours, sacrificed relationships, and committed myself to making my ideas become realities. So competition didn't scare me away.

If you let the competition scare you, you won't survive. Instead, you should let the competition be the adrenaline that keeps you going. Beating out your competition should be the reason you get out of bed in the morning. When you step out and start selling, it will be time to see just how big the fight inside you really is.

Make Them Sell to You

Most people think "selling" is the same as "talking." But the most effective salespeople know that listening is the most important part of their job.

— Roy Bartell

If you really want to know what a client needs from you, sit down with them and just be quiet. Listen. Let them tell you their life story because people love to talk. People will tell you how smart they are, stories about their kids, how much money they've made and what it is they're doing. And if you listen just long enough, that client will actually do all the hard sales work for you. They'll sell the product themselves, because if you let them talk, they will tell you exactly what it is they need. All that's left to do is fill their need with your product and close the sale.

There will also be times when that issue of integrity comes up again. There will be instances when it's easier to compromise your integrity to land a big sale. But remember, that will haunt you for years to come. So don't do it, no matter how tempting it is, or how bad you need the money. It's not worth it.

It's All About The Relationship

Sales is all about building relationships, but you won't like every client you work with. Some may be crooks and some may be saints. The point is, you're going to have to work with a variety of different people who have a lot of different personalities, and you're going to have to find a way to work with each and every one.

One of the biggest mistakes people make when they are

getting started in business is not knowing how to work with dishonest and somewhat unlikeable people.

When I was running the aggregate business, I did my best to learn as much about the people I did business with as possible. I took note of every little thing about their business and personal lives, because for a lot of people, the two aren't easily separated. The carryover from how they conduct their personal lives will give you a good idea of how they will succeed (or fail) in their business lives.

For example, there was this one guy in particular I held to a very low credit limit of $2,500 because of his lavish and unsavory lifestyle. On several occasions, he sent his manager, Jim, over to try to persuade me to raise his credit limit, but I wouldn't do it.

You see, Jim's boss had a knack for spending money like a drunken sailor on Saturday night. He showered his wife and mistresses in clothes, cars, jewelry and anything else they had a whim for on a regular basis. I hope you noticed I said mistresses, because he always had more than one. He was the kind of guy who always had to have more than one of everything. His company always suffered because of his first and only priority in life, which was self-indulgence to the extreme.

He and Jim both wore my door out trying to get me to raise his credit limit to fifty thousand dollars, but I wouldn't budge. I never raised his limit from the original $2,500 even though we did business for several years. It was my money on the line, so I wouldn't raise it up knowing our priorities with money didn't line up. And I knew they didn't line up because I saw the carryover from the way he mismanaged his personal life.

I worried day and night about leverage, and he worried day and night about cleavage.

Needless to say his story ended ugly (for him). He went broke three years later and now drives a truck for a living to this very day. I maintained a solid business relationship with him right up until the day he lost his business. I didn't have a personal relationship with the guy. He lacked the integrity I usually look for in a friend. But I learned how to have a business relationship with him on my terms.

Integrity Still Counts

I know I've said don't do deals that will cost you your integrity. But I didn't say, "Don't do business with crooks." If you are only going to do business with honest people, you'll see that the field is extremely limited. There are a lot of dishonest people out there who need your product or services. Doing business with dishonest people is different than doing dishonest deals.

Of course, you will have to be careful when you're selling your products and services to people who have shady reputations. If you don't learn to read the situation and the people in it, you're going to be defeated, plain and simple, because knowing your product and knowing your market is never enough.

It's survival of the fittest, and the fittest are always the ones who hone their intuitive skills of observation and listening.

I'm talking about integrity here again in this section because I know that when times get tough, it's easy to want to loosen up on the reigns of your integrity. You might be tempted to say your product does something it doesn't do. You might be tempted to say you can provide it at a cost you can't provide. You might be tempted to guarantee things you can't back up. Don't do it.

When it comes to sales, there are four tenets I live by: integrity in my product, integrity in my pitch, integrity in my delivery, and integrity in my warranty.

If you want to be the most successful at sales, be known for delivering the best product at a fair price, on time, every time, to the best of your ability. And be willing to stand behind your promise.

Let THAT be your reputation, and you won't have to worry about sales.

Action Steps:

Commit to memory these important sales tenets:

1. Integrity in your product.

2. Integrity in your pitch.

3. Integrity in your delivery

4. Integrity in your warranty.

The Take Away:

Always approach your customers with a goal of establishing a win-win relationship.

CHAPTER NINE

GROWING YOUR BUSINESS

"You've got to find ways to improve and expand your business, if for no other reason than to keep yourself focused and interested in what you're doing."

— Robert S. Lott

Henry Hershey was an entrepreneur, but as far as entrepreneurs go, he was a terrible one. He dragged his family from town to town chasing one crazy business idea after another, contributing to the fact that his son, Milton, managed to obtain only a 4th grade education. The one thing Henry Hershey lacked was the work ethic required to stick with a business idea when the work became hard.

Finally tired of his nonsense, Hershey's wife, Fanny, took her son, Milton, back to their home in Lancaster, Pennsylvania, where she instilled in him the work ethic his father lacked.

Milton Hershey, however, like his father, had an entrepreneur's spirit. After several missteps in his entrepreneurial career, Hershey started the Lancaster Caramel Company.

He took out a loan, using his Aunt Maddie's home as collateral, and was given 90 days to pay back the $700 loan. Despite the incredible taste and well-received support of the locals, Hershey didn't make enough to pay back the money and the bank called the loan.

Hershey, undaunted and driven with passion for his product, went to the bank and said, "I can't pay back the $700, and I need even more money to buy more ingredients."[4] He took the bank's loan officer with him, a man whom he'd built a relationship with, and convinced him of the viability of the business.

Seventeen years later, he sold his caramel company for 1 million dollars (a 2014 equivalent of roughly $28 million dollars) and started the Hershey Chocolate Company.

---

4. "Hershey Biography." Bio.com. January 20, 2008. Accessed February 9, 2015. http://www.biography.com/people/milton-hershey-9337133#synopsis.

GROWING YOUR BUSINESS

It is an inevitable plight of the entrepreneur to fail, more than likely, many, many times. It's why I've talked so much about having the resolve, the grit, and the determination to keep working hard, to get back up when you get knocked down, to spit the blood out of our mouth and go another round. Eventually, if you work hard enough and smart enough, your business is going to need room to grow.

You have to be ready for this. You've got to find ways to improve and expand your business, if for no other reason than to keep yourself focused and interested in what you're doing.

Did you know that Milton Hershey discovered caramel as an apprentice at a job he hated? And the only reason he was even working as an apprentice in a caramel shop is because his previous business venture went straight up bankrupt.

Did you know he discovered chocolate at the U.S. World's Fair while still building his caramel business? Figuring out where your business will go next will keep you sharp because you'll be thinking of new ideas and looking for new opportunities. Your employees will respect you for getting out there and hustling too.

Moving a Company to the Next Level — Physically & Mentally

Entrepreneurs tend to think that the next level is a huge quantum leap forward—that the next step will take them where they need to be. The reality is that there are a lot of next levels in business and life, and you should view them as nothing more than stair steps. They are an even progression of height, a step up, a step up, a step up. They are not that grand leap that most people envision.

If it is some superman mentality that you're striving for, remember that it's made of many small steps, not a giant leap. Michael Jordan wasn't drafted number one, and nobody had a clue that Michael Jordan was going to become THE Michael Jordan. Michael Jordan didn't even make his high school basketball team becasue he was too short and too inexperienced. But he was determined to play, and to be the best. So he learned all he could by watching his friends play, and when his time came, he proved he had what it took. He evolved one small step at a time, over a period of time, until eventually he was playing professional ball.

When you understand that those steps are small, you will look forward to progressing up each level. You won't look way across 5,000 miles of open water and think that all you've got is a paddle. It's not like that. Mentally make positive steps in the right direction over a period of time.

That's how people and companies grow physically and mentally.

Learn How to Deal with "No"

If you really want to become a passionate business owner, you have to learn how to hear the word "No" and just move on. So many people I know are afraid to be told "No," and that's just ridiculous. You can't sit in your office and hope someone magically comes along who loves you and all of your ideas so much they want to throw money at you. The only place where that could happen would be in your imagination. It's just not going to happen in the real world of business. People who sit around waiting for some big investor to fund their dreams are either fools, lazy, or a combination of both. If you're not ready to be told "No," then you're not ready to be in business.

Don't get all wrapped up in thinking the people who are telling you "No" are doing it to hurt you. It's just business. If you've got something you think is a great prospect, but no one else seems to think so, that's a sign something's got to change. That's all. The idea and the business might be great, but maybe the way you're pitching it to the bank is the problem. Figure it out and adapt. Learn from every situation, adjust, and move on down the road. Every "No" you hear gets you one step closer to a "Yes."

Knock on 1,000 Doors

Most people don't really know how to push and ask enough for what they want. Do you know how many banks I went to before I found a guy to do business with me? More than 20. I told the story so many times I got tired of telling it. Finally, I managed to tell it to a guy who listened to me. He said, "I'll do that." I kept talking, like a scene from a comedy. I looked at him and he looked at me like, "Seriously, you can shut up now. I said I would do it."

All I could come back with was, "Seriously? What did you just say?"

"I think that's something we can look at, and I think I have a way that I can show you how to do it."

You just have to knock on enough doors, and someone will eventually say yes. It may be 10 doors, maybe 100, or you may knock on 1,000 doors. But I promise you that if you ask and you push enough, you will get what you are looking for. Eventually, God will get tired of hearing you talk about it. He'll say, "Okay, you wanted it. Here it is, go do something with it."

How (and when) to Deal with Banks

You're going to want to gloss right over this section, but I'm telling you, this is information that will be vital to the success of your business. Banks and bankers require some understanding. Ninety-nine percent of bankers like the low-hanging fruit and the sure deals. They like to loan people money that don't really need any money. If they bring a loan into the bank and it doesn't perform, they'll face some severe consequences and no one wants to stick their neck out for you. So if a banker says "No" that doesn't mean your business plan is bad or won't work. It just may be at that particular time he has several loans that are in trouble, and he doesn't need any more new startups that he has to pitch to his loan committee.

Don't get me wrong, bankers will go out on a limb to help get a new business off of the ground, but the timing has to be right. If a bank is in the process of taking a write-off on some losses, then the chances of you being given an audience will be very slim. So don't let "No" change the goal you've set. **That "No" is the bank's "No." It's not a merit evaluation of you or your business plan.**

When I was young I can't tell you how many times I was humiliated by bankers time and again, but I just kept knocking on doors. In those days, they were really coarse about it. They would just look at me and say, "Really? Are you serious? In your wildest imagination, how does that work?" Bankers wouldn't spare your feelings back then like they do now. They would tell you right quick what they really thought without much concern.

Today things are a bit different in the banking world,

so when it comes to dealing with bankers, you want to remember a few things:

1. **Know When to Talk to a Banker**

    If you want an edge on talking to bankers, you need to find out what day is loan committee day. Whatever you do, never go talk to a guy after a loan committee meeting because there's a big chance he's been chewed out. It's best to talk to bankers in the morning, preferably after they've had a cup of coffee and they're fresh. Don't ever talk to a banker late in the afternoon or right after a board meeting. They're just frazzled and distracted, and that's not the type of mindset you need when you're trying to pitch an idea for funding. Set things up so that "Yes" will happen.

2. **Develop a Relationship with Your Banker**

    There are some key points to remember about bankers and this holds true for the present and until the end of time. And when I say "remember," I mean never in your wildest imagination think it will ever be any different for one second.

    The first thing is they never have and never will be your friend. When I say build a great relationship with your banker, I am talking in the business sense. They are running a business and making business decisions, so don't expect any kind of special treatment. Their decisions are based on your performance and assets, nothing else. Their down-home-we're-all-neighbors persona is like the fancy office and monogramed shirts; it's just part of the bank's landscape.

The second thing to remember is the most important. Bankers are NOT qualified to run a business, not even a snow cone stand on a hot beach. Their only qualification in life is to loan money according to their bank's guidelines. They are all armchair quarterbacks that dispense business advice like it's the Holy Grail. They supply money—that's it, money that is the fuel for your race team, the end. They can't even start the car much less devise the strategy of how to avoid crashes and win races. So when they start that philosophy of theirs, just remember, if they had the skill set or guts for the race, you would see them in the driver's seat instead of the cheap seats.

That said, having a great relationship with your banker will do wonders for improving your chances of getting a loan. Be honest with your bankers at all times. If they know they can trust you, they'll be more likely to want to loan you money!

3. **Be Prepared to Change Banks**

    One time I wanted to borrow a substantial amount of money to fund a big project, so I went to my banker and presented my loan request. I got him on a bad day or at the wrong time of day and he said, "Hey look, you really need to find another bank. We're not interested in the loan and really not that interested in your business anymore." I left the bank shocked at being treated so harshly.

    Anyway, my banker left on vacation for a couple of weeks, and I went to work finding a new bank. I applied for a loan with another bank and was approved while he was on vacation. Several weeks after he came back, my new bank called him for my payoffs. He called me all upset and asked me to come to the bank, which I did.

    By taking my business somewhere else, I made him look bad in front of his loan directors. He started to raise hell right there in the bank, and

I told him "You told me I needed to find a new bank and that's what I did." He went off the rails and commenced to giving me a cussing, so I reached across his desk and grabbed him by his tie. I never will forget it because it had some goofy little red designs on it and without thinking, I jerked him across his desk. Needless to say things got a little western. I was asked to leave the bank, which I did with great embarrassment. I was embarrassed over being asked to leave but not for jerking him across his desk (because he really deserved more than I gave him). That was back in my dumber days, and I certainly don't recommend you behave that way, but I think the guy got my point.

To this day though, I keep a little bit of business at a couple of banks, just in case I need to make a change.

4. **The Bank Can't Finance Your Business Plan, No Matter How Great You Think It Is**

Governmental banking regulations forbid banks from loaning money on business plans. It's not because the government wants to discourage small business owners. It's because they have to protect the depositors who put their money in the banks all across the country. They can only loan you money if you have assets you can put up as collateral to secure the bank's position should your business fail. The Small Business Administration is the answer for a lot of new startups that don't have hard assets to pledge against a loan. The government will guarantee up to 70% of a loan for a new startup, which gives the bank an incentive to approve your loan. It's why it's important to have a good relationship with your banker so they'll be willing to participate in a Small Business Administration loan request (and why you shouldn't jerk him over his desk).

Understanding how to grow your business into a successful, moneymaking endeavor is like climbing a mountain. You have to be intentional about every step of the process, and continue to be willing to take step after step after step toward the top.

Action Steps:

You have one simple action step to take for this chapter. I'm not asking you to look across the ocean at 5,000 miles of open water. I'm asking you to look forward to the next step you need to take to grow your business.

What is that ONE next step?

The Take Away:

Move forward with thought-out precision, not speed.

CHAPTER TEN

AVOIDING THE PITFALLS

*"Talent and hard work will always produce results.
Just remember, those results are quantifiable; so
manage with that thought."*

— Robert S. Lott

There was a long period of time when no one wanted
to enter the ring with Mike Tyson. The power behind
his fists was too much for competitors, and he won
his first 19 professional fights by knockout. Mike Tyson was
a blend of brute strength and natural talent. At the ripe age
of 20, "Iron Mike" was the world's youngest heavyweight
champ.

It's estimated that Tyson earned well over 400 million

dollars boxing in his prime. But in the late 1990s, when he was at the peak of his professional career, a string of events, including the infamous bite of Evander Holyfield's ear, began to strain his career. He spent everything he worked so hard to earn.

Cars, mansions, and exotic animals mixed with a costly divorce resulted in bankruptcy for Tyson. In 2003, it was said his debt amounted to around 27 million dollars. "Iron Mike" couldn't fight his way out of the consequences of his poor decisions, and the fact of the matter is no one can.

It takes so much work to get a business on its feet, much less to turn it into a moneymaking venture, so understanding how you can derail your own success is an important part of learning about business. I've seen a lot of men destroy their chances of success because they fall into three common business pitfalls: they like their toys, they can't say no to their kids, and they can't adapt to change.

The Pitfalls of Temptation

With success comes a bit of temptation, and temptation doesn't care who you are or what you believe in; it knocks on everyone's door. As soon as Tyson started to earn his money, he started to spend it on things he didn't need. Tyson's business was in his fists, but there weren't enough fights for him to win to keep up with his outlandish spending habits. The more he earned, the more he needed. And, this same temptation trap has taken down more than its fair share of successful business owners.

I've seen some really smart guys fail because they couldn't control two things: how they spent their money and how they spent their time.

It doesn't matter how much money you make and what business legacy you may leave behind if you carelessly throw away everything you have on things that don't matter. Former millionaires filing bankruptcy simply because they couldn't resist the temptation to buy more things is inexcusable. Your legacy shouldn't be that you were a businessman who had to have everything; your legacy should be that you used your iron will in business to do things that matter.

Outside of the risk of just flat out running out of money, you also need to control your urge to spend for the morale of your company. When your employees watch you use your money to buy meaningless stuff, it starts to eat away at them. They come in every day, work hard, but don't have the luxury of purchasing big-ticket support items that the company needs to stay competitive. Your excessive lifestyle will start to breed negative feelings in your employees, and in turn, it will affect how they work or IF they will choose to work for you any longer at all. Talented people have options, so if you run your company with more focus on the things you can buy and less on how to take care of the company and those who work for it, you'll find yourself working alone.

Money isn't the only thing you can waste. Time is money - for you, your employees, your family, and other business owners. You can tell a lot about a person based on how they spend their time. It's a precious commodity with a limited amount, so if someone spends a lot of time with their focus on other things, then their focus isn't on making their business more successful. This is where a lot of entrepreneurs get complacent and lose their edge.

I had a friend that owned a really nice little company, and he was a brilliant businessman with years of experience and a personality that made you feel instantly at ease. But he had a passion for baseball that outweighed his passion for growing a business. He would sit down and talk my ear off about baseball players' batting averages, strikeout percentages, and how much they were paid. Every year when baseball season started, he put his business on autopilot because baseball consumed his life, totally. He always had a nice little business, but it stayed just that - little. He got his bills paid, but everyone in his industry knew where his priorities lay. It always has been and always will be baseball for him.

But as you are reading this, I want to caution you: don't be too quick to judge. People lose their way every day for a variety of reasons. The point here is to always keep the needle pointed to true north, and when it's not, have the guts to change it. The only thing that will change that needle is self-examination and taking action. The guys that are the toughest competitors are the ones that keep a tight check on their true north needle and react quickly with the right corrections.

In my book, *On Target*, I talk about specific ways to make sure your needle is always pointing to true north, and how to keep temptation from taking over. Remember that target I had you draw in your action steps in Chapter Four? That's what I use to keep me mentally focused and from giving into temptation. Of course I go into more detail in the book, but the rings on my target are composed of myself, my family, my faith, my personal health, and my finances. I keep control of my life by making sure the things that get my time and my money are in those rings.

Setting limits on yourself will help keep your priorities in check. It will help your family and employees respect you. And ultimately, it will save your business.

The Pitfalls of Business Heirs

Another pitfall business owner's face is how they pass on their company to their children. Business owners need to have a plan in place for what will happen to the business if something happens to them or as they get closer to retirement. Harvard Business Review reported only 30% of businesses succeed after being passed on to the next generation. There's a simple solution to this pitfall: don't pass along your company unless your kid has proven he or she has the passion, the guts, and the leadership to take it on.

Ever heard the expression, "No guts, no glory?" I know an entrepreneur whose son wanted all the glory without having to put in any guts. All of the distractions he had growing up with money left him without a college education and with no focus. His father gave him a high-level position in his business despite the fact that he knew very little about running a business. There are literally hundreds of businesses owners that have this one stupid business decision in common.

Just because your children have your last name doesn't mean they have your skill set to start or run a business of any size. I am always amazed how entrepreneurs think that their children have the most important asset they will ever need in life and that's their last name.

For kids who grow up in families of wealth, if they aren't forced to learn the wage of a hard day's work, they just don't understand the value of a dollar. Watch how kids behave who have money; everything is disposable because they aren't the ones paying for it. Well, if they behave like that with their stuff, what makes you think they will treat your business any different?

Second-generation owners usually don't succeed because they either aren't qualified for the position or they are forced into it. If your kid wants to be part of the family business, they need to earn it. My daughter worked hard and proved her worth when she worked for me. She wasn't given anything just because of her last name. My son was the same way because I demanded it. You'll be able to recognize if your kid is going to be able to run your company because you'll see the same attributes you had when you were just starting out: hard-working, honest, and full of passion.

If you see those traits in your child and they express an interest to take over the company, you've got to invest in them. You've got to show them the ropes. For a smooth transition, let them run the company for a while with you still there, take them on appointments with you to meet clients, and let them have an opportunity to build up their own reputation. You can use that time to see if you've picked the right replacement and when you leave, you can rest a little easier. But just to be safe, make sure you have a good cash foundation under the business in case things don't work out as planned.

On the other hand, if your kid doesn't show any interest, don't push them. Instead, lend a helping hand to find out what does interest them and help them create opportunities to find their own success.

And lastly, if your kid is interested in taking over your company but just isn't a good fit, you have to be honest with them. It's not personal, it's business. And in a business, there are lots of people who rely on continued success of the company. So even if your child wants to run the company, if you don't think they know the ropes well enough to do so, let them know they always have a place in your family, but that doesn't mean they always have a place in the company.

The Pitfalls of Change

The last area where I see young entrepreneurs fail is in adapting to change. When you've been in business as long as I have, you see things change. Society, technology, government regulations, and even the process of starting a company has drastically changed since I started. As a business owner, you can't afford to fear change; you have to embrace it and adapt to it. Dealing with change can determine whether or not a business makes it through the years or sinks like a stone in a river.

In my opinion, the best change that's ever happened to this country and the world over is the opportunity for anyone to start a business today. It doesn't matter if you're a woman, a man, a minority, or if you're young or old, you can start a business. This means ideas are more diverse and competition is tighter. Both of those things force businesses to be better. And businesses that can't keep up with such societal changes go under.

Advances in technology have also drastically changed how we do business. I remember feeling like a big shot for having a phone in my company truck years and years ago. If you don't have a cell phone in today's society, you're the odd man out. Equipment is more efficient. Computers are everywhere, and everyone seems to know how to use them. The Internet allows you to access loads of information at any time of the day from anywhere in the world. Everything moves at a lightning pace, and if you don't keep up with the pace of technology and learn how to properly incorporate technology into your business you'll get flat run over.

And while I'm talking about the advantages of technology, let me remind you of some of the pitfalls.

1. **We aren't able to draw a definite line between work life and home life.**

    Technology allows us to bring our work with us everywhere we go. It's important to have boundaries with your employees, clients, and your family when it comes to work. I always advise people to turn off the technology when they get home and focus their time and energy on the people they don't get to see very often.

2. **It increases our chance of burnout.**

   It's important for you to step away from your business to avoid getting stuck on a bad idea and the risk of burning yourself out. Stepping away from the computer, turning off the cell phone, and focusing on your family allows your brain to rest and reset.

The biggest setback we have today (in my humble opinion) is all the government regulations mucking up the gears of good business. When I started out, if you had an idea and the money to back it up, all you had to do was get your permits from the local courthouse and get to work. Don't get me wrong, it's important for the government to step in and take care of resources and regulate how businesses are operated, but there are so many regulations out there you'll need to stay informed.

The best business owners not only understand that change is going to happen, but they embrace it. Change isn't easy, but most of the time it's worth it. As the owner, your job is to make transitions, no matter what they are, as smooth as possible. Ben Franklin said it best: "When you're finished changing, you're finished."

Keep your head above water, keep your spending under control, and keep the right people running your business, and your business will continue to grow and thrive.

Action Steps:

1. Describe a time when you have let your desire to have "things" cloud your good sense. How did you get out of the mess you created?

2. What do you spend the majority of your time on? Is it work, is it social media, family? Make a bar graph that illustrates how you spend your week. Include hobbies, work, meetings, social media, family time, and friend time.

The Take Away:

Business doesn't get easier as time goes by. You have to always be on your "A" game, no matter how long you're in business.

EPILOGUE

DON'T BE THAT GUY

I n closing, I'd like to share a story that was told to me many years ago concerning our God-given talents. The origin of the yarn was supposedly one of Mark Twain's favorite stories that he told frequently.

There was once a professor who studied the art of war with a great fascination, especially concerning all of the great military leaders. Over the years, there were many heated debates within his academic circles as to who had the best military mind for all of the ages. Some argued Napoleon, some Genghis Kahn, and others the great Generals of the Roman Empire, but there was never a clear consensus on anyone.

Well the professor up and died one day and went to

heaven. After St. Peter finished showing him around, he asked the professor if he had any questions. The professor said he did, just one.

St. Peter stopped and said, "Ask."

The professor was beside himself. "Of all of the great military geniuses, who was the best?"

St. Peter smiled and looked around for a moment then pointed to a man sitting under a shade tree.

The professor stared at the man in disbelief. "That can't be. I know that man. He never did anything accept odd jobs around our town."

St. Peter said, "I know. You asked who had the best military mind." St. Peter could see the confusion on the professor's face. Then he added, "He was given a very unique talent; he just decided not to use it."

So don't deprive yourself, your family, and mankind of your unique talent.

AND REMEMBER!!! All talents are small seeds that need to be planted. To my knowledge, I've never seen a farmer plant anything while sitting on a couch. So get up and get serious about success.

ROBERT S. LOTT